# Ten F<br>for Br̶e̶a̶s̶t̶

ex libris

Candlestick Press

Published by:
Candlestick Press,
Diversity House, 72 Nottingham Road, Arnold, Nottingham UK NG5 6LF
www.candlestickpress.co.uk

Design and typesetting by Diversity Creative Marketing Solutions Ltd.,
www.diversity.agency

Printed by Ratcliff & Roper Print Group, Nottinghamshire, UK

Selection and Introduction © Ana Sampson 2019

Cover illustration © Jane Walker 2018
www.janewalkerprintmaker.com

Candlestick Press monogram © Barbara Shaw, 2008

© Candlestick Press, 2019

ISBN 978 1 907598 72 2

**Acknowledgements:**

The poems in this pamphlet are reprinted from the following books, all by
permission of the publishers listed unless stated otherwise. Every effort has
been made to trace the copyright holders of the poems published in this book.
The editor and publisher apologise if any material has been included without
permission or without the appropriate acknowledgement, and would be glad
to be told of anyone who has not been consulted. Thanks are due to all the
copyright holders cited below for their kind permission:

Elizabeth Bishop, *Poems* (FSG, 2011) by permission of A. M. Heath and
Farrar, Straus and Giroux. Billy Collins, *Picnic, Lightning* (University of
Pittsburgh Press, 1994) © 1994 reprinted by permission of University of
Pittsburgh Press. Elizabeth Daryush, *The Last Man & Other Verses* (Carcanet
Press, 1936). Ted Kooser, *Weather Central* (University of Pittsburgh Press,
1994) © 1994 reprinted by permission of University of Pittsburgh Press.
Lani O'Hanlon, *Hallelujah for 50ft Women* (Bloodaxe Books, 2015) by kind
permission of the author. Charles Simic, *The Book of Gods and Devils*
(Harcourt Brace Jovanovich, 1990) © 1990 by Charles Simic. Reprinted by
permission of Houghton Mifflin Harcourt Publishing Company. All rights
reserved. Mary Stewart Hammond, in *Out of Canaan* (W. W. Norton, 1991)
Copyright © 1991 by Mary Stewart Hammond. Originally appeared in The
New Yorker. Used by permission of W. W. Norton & Company, Inc. All rights
reserved. Olga Dermott-Bond, poem as yet unpublished, by kind permission
of the author. Phil M Houghton, poem as yet unpublished, by kind
permission of the author. Catherine Edmunds, poem as yet unpublished, by
kind permission of the author.

All permissions cleared courtesy of Swift Permissions
(swiftpermissions@gmail.com).

Where poets are no longer living, their dates are given.

# Introduction

I am far from a natural early riser, but a few years of being thrust, blinking, into dawnscapes by small children has at last convinced me of morning's pleasures. From the vantage point of daybreak, once the coffee pot has done her vital work, the day stretches before us. What possibilities it holds! What acres of achievement seem to lie within our grasp today, once we have broken bread!

I could have laid a table five times this size with delicious morning poems, but here is a breakfast buffet – is there any more delightful phrase? – composed of my very favourites. I'm especially thrilled that the entries to Candlestick Press's breakfast competition were so wonderful – frequently tender, often thought-provoking, all demanding to be savoured – that I chose to include three of them instead of the planned two.

We slip from the sheets with Billy Collins, knocking back espresso and flexing our fingers ready for the day's work. Between the lines of 'Breakfast with Mother', a whole delicately agonising novel is spun across the table, between the sugar bowl and brittle teacups. Elizabeth Daryush's 'Still Life' allows us to glide for a moment into a deliciously opulent morning, worlds away from the frenetic dash of most of mine and all the more nourishing for it. Lani O'Hanlon finds moments for contemplation over a hen-warm egg, while Elizabeth Bishop spies grand palaces in a sunlit crumb.

We have eaten now, and fortified ourselves. In the final three beautiful poems, we push out into the bird-filled air of the morning. We are the first to walk the world. The day spreads before us and is not spoilt yet.

I wish you good mornings and big breakfasts. May your dawns be rosy and your coffee always hot.

*Ana Sampson*

# Morning

Why do we bother with the rest of the day,
the swale of the afternoon,
the sudden dip into evening,

then night with his notorious perfumes,
his many-pointed stars?

This is the best—
throwing off the light covers,
feet on the cold floor,
and buzzing around the house on espresso—

maybe a splash of water on the face,
a palmful of vitamins—
but mostly buzzing around the house on espresso,

dictionary and atlas open on the rug,
the typewriter waiting for the key of the head,
a cello on the radio,

and, if necessary, the windows—
trees fifty, a hundred years old
out there,
heavy clouds on the way
and the lawn steaming like a horse
in the early morning.


*Billy Collins*

# Toaster

Each Sunday morning
the bread would often get stuck
or launch itself high

across the kitchen
where dad would catch it, juggling
each flapping bird with

blackened wings. His dance
made us laugh. Tea, marmalade,
homemade jam, honey –

again and again
we would wait for its metalled
cough, to watch salmon

leaping through currents
of sun. I ate six slices
one weekend, enthralled

with how happiness
was the colour of butter,
best eaten hot. Toast.

I believed I could
save each tiny crumb of you,
thinking aged just four

that every Sunday
would stay like this, love landing
soft, the right way up.


*Olga Dermott-Bond*

# Breakfast with Mother

Margaret Penfold rises early, fine in her intent, but she
will never be court painter to the Elector Palatine
in Düsseldorf, any more than a chronicler of dissolute life.

She is breakfasting with her mother, they live in Maidenhead,
and thus she cannot be Hogarth, and nor is she destined to be
a forgotten female pioneer of the Bauhaus; not permitted

to be surreal, she will never paint a world of soft watches
and sex. Grey dawn breaks, a thin, silver line of a faraway war,
a young man, his split lens goggles, the scent of leather,

that day on the Downs, but an image of dead horses, filled
with maggots comes unbidden; she wrenches her thoughts
to a graceful image; warm flowers in a glass vase, one tulip.

Mother looks up from her paper, says the rest of the month
could have cold spells, and oh look, they've dragged
a model Ichthyosaurus out of its pond in the grounds

of Crystal Palace. Margaret doesn't listen, consumed by
the danger of hope, the awkwardness of grief. There are
different sorts of confusion and she has been on a journey,

far removed from the fragranced linen of home, from this
wretched commission which will damn her before it saves her:
a small boy, kneeling, in his arms a soft grey rabbit,

while birds in a tree hold forbidden conversations, faking
righteousness in the sight of God—but there are asterisks
in her diary. They signify naught, should Mother think to ask.


*Catherine Edmunds*

## Still-Life

Through the open French window the warm sun
lights up the polished breakfast-table, laid
round a bowl of crimson roses, for one –
a service of Worcester porcelain, arrayed
near it a melon, peaches, figs, small hot
rolls in a napkin, fairy rack of toast,
butter in ice, high silver coffee pot,
and, heaped on a salver, the morning's post.

She comes over the lawn, the young heiress,
from her early walk in her garden-wood
feeling that life's a table set to bless
her delicate desires with all that's good,

that even the unopened future lies
like a love-letter, full of sweet surprise.


*Elizabeth Daryush (1887 – 1977)*

## Cherry Blossoms

Barefoot, I walk to the hen house,
lift the door – reach
into a sanctuary of straw,
find the egg warm
in the cup of my hand.

The new hen still cuckling,
I drop the egg into a pot of water,
butter toast, measure time.

Everything stops as I eat,
my stale thoughts and musty breath,

and I remember
Ellie Byrne and me
looking up through cherry blossoms
at stars and the young night,

our warm round bellies,
before the eggs
began to fall.


*Lani O'Hanlon*

## Making Breakfast

There's this ritual, like a charm,
Southern women do after their men
make love to them in the morning.
We rush to the kitchen. As if possessed.
Make one of those big breakfasts
from the old days. To say thank you.
When we know we shouldn't. Understanding
the act smacks of Massah, looks shuffly as
all getout, adds to his belly, which is bad
for his back, and will probably give him
cancer, cardiac arrest, and a stroke. So,
you do have to wonder these days as you
get out the fat-back, knead the dough,
adjust the flame for a slow boil,
flick water on the cast-iron skillet
to check if it's ready and the kitchen
gets steamy and close and smelling
to high heaven, if this isn't an act
of aggressive hostility and/or a symptom
of regressed tractability. Although
on the days we don't I am careful
about broiling his meats instead of
deep-fat frying them for a couple of hours,
dipped in flour, serving them smothered
in cream gravy made from the drippings,
and, in fact, I won't even do
that anymore period, no matter what
he does to deserve it, and besides, we are
going on eighteen years so it's not as if we
eat breakfast as often as we used to,
and when we do I now should serve him –
forget the politics of who serves whom –
oatmeal after? But if this drive answers
to days when death, like woolly mammoths
and Visigoth hordes and rebellious kinsmen,
waited outside us, then it's healthy, if

primitive, to cook Southern. Consider it
an extra precaution. I look at his face,
that weak-kneed, that buffalo-eyed,
Samson-after-his-haircut face, all of him
burnished with grits and sausage
and fried apples and biscuits and my
power, and adrift outside himself,
and the sight makes me feel all over
again like what I thank him for
except bigger, slower, lasting, as if,
hog-tied, the hunk of him were risen
with the splotchy butterfly on my chest,
which, contrary to medical opinion, does not
fade but lifts off into the atmosphere,
coupling, going on ahead.


*Mary Stewart Hammond*

## A Miracle for Breakfast

At six o'clock we were waiting for coffee,
waiting for coffee and the charitable crumb
that was going to be served from a certain balcony,
—like kings of old, or like a miracle.
It was still dark. One foot of the sun
steadied itself on a long ripple in the river.

The first ferry of the day had just crossed the river.
It was so cold we hoped that the coffee
would be very hot, seeing that the sun
was not going to warm us; and that the crumb
would be a loaf each, buttered, by a miracle.
At seven a man stepped out on the balcony.

He stood for a minute alone on the balcony
looking over our heads toward the river.
A servant handed him the makings of a miracle,
consisting of one lone cup of coffee
and one roll, which he proceeded to crumb,
his head, so to speak, in the clouds—along with the sun.

Was the man crazy? What under the sun
was he trying to do, up there on his balcony!
Each man received one rather hard crumb,
which some flicked scornfully into the river,
and, in a cup, one drop of the coffee.
Some of us stood around, waiting for the miracle.

I can tell what I saw next; it was not a miracle.
A beautiful villa stood in the sun
and from its doors came the smell of hot coffee.
In front, a baroque white plaster balcony
added by birds, who nest along the river,
—I saw it with one eye close to the crumb—

and galleries and marble chambers. My crumb
my mansion, made for me by a miracle,
through ages, by insects, birds, and the river
working the stone. Every day, in the sun,
at breakfast time I sit on my balcony
with my feet up, and drink gallons of coffee.

We licked up the crumb and swallowed the coffee.
A window across the river caught the sun
as if the miracle were working, on the wrong balcony.


*Elizabeth Bishop (1911 – 1979)*

## Heights of Folly

O crows circling over my head and cawing!
I admit to being, at times,
Suddenly, and without the slightest warning,
Exceedingly happy.

On a morning otherwise sunless,
Strolling arm in arm
Past some gallows-shaped trees
With my dear Helen,
Who is also a strange bird.

A feeling of being summoned
Urgently, but by a most gracious invitation
To breakfast on slices of watermelon
In the company of naked gods and goddesses
On a patch of last night's snow.


*Charles Simic*

## Before the lark

leave me
in the company
of doorsteps
carve up the pavement
with thin shafts of light
take in the milk
without a word
for I am walking
with the dawn
sweeping cobwebs
from its face
and *this* is the morning
and *I* am the first

before the streets are aired


*Phil M Houghton*

*Final line: a saying of my Grandad; an early riser and whom I never met*

**Poem Before Breakfast**

A small brown bird flies toward me
over the pond, ferrying light
on its back, on its gliding wings,
bearing up part of the morning,

a small brown part—merely a flake
of significance, really, in all
the world of light around it,
blue, yellow, and green, yet

perfectly cared for, perfectly
tended, one piece of a moment
borne skillfully over the water,
and I blessed to receive it.


*Ted Kooser*